# VEROTCHKA'S TALES



ILLUSTRATED BY
BORIS M.
ARTZYBASHEFF

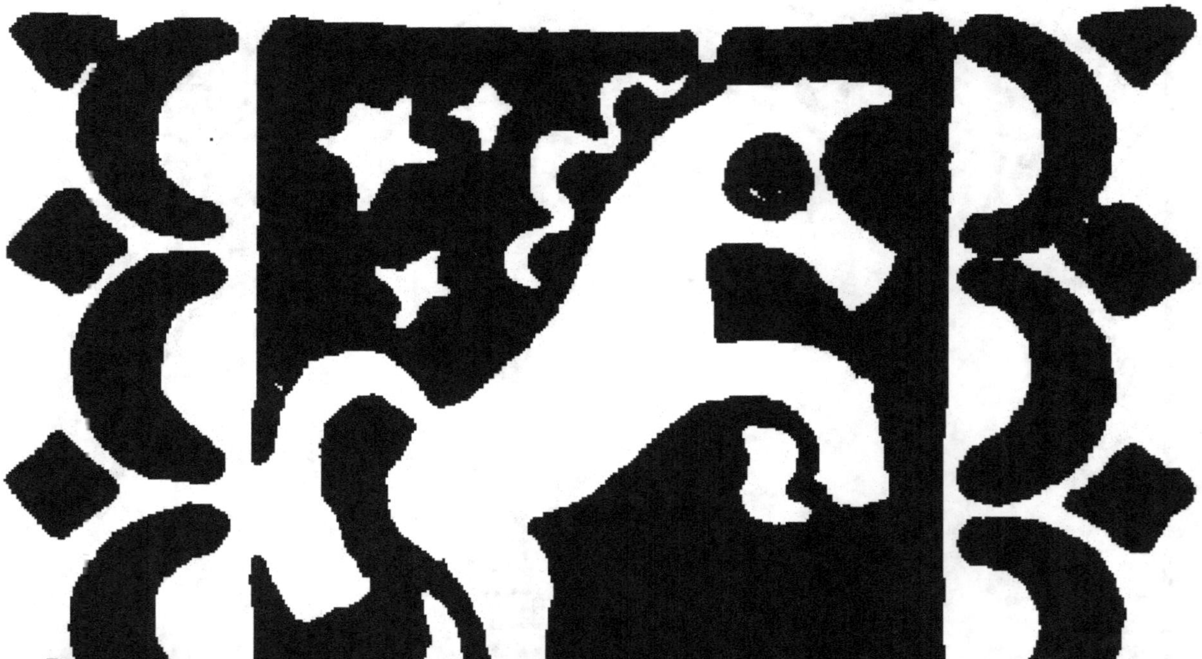

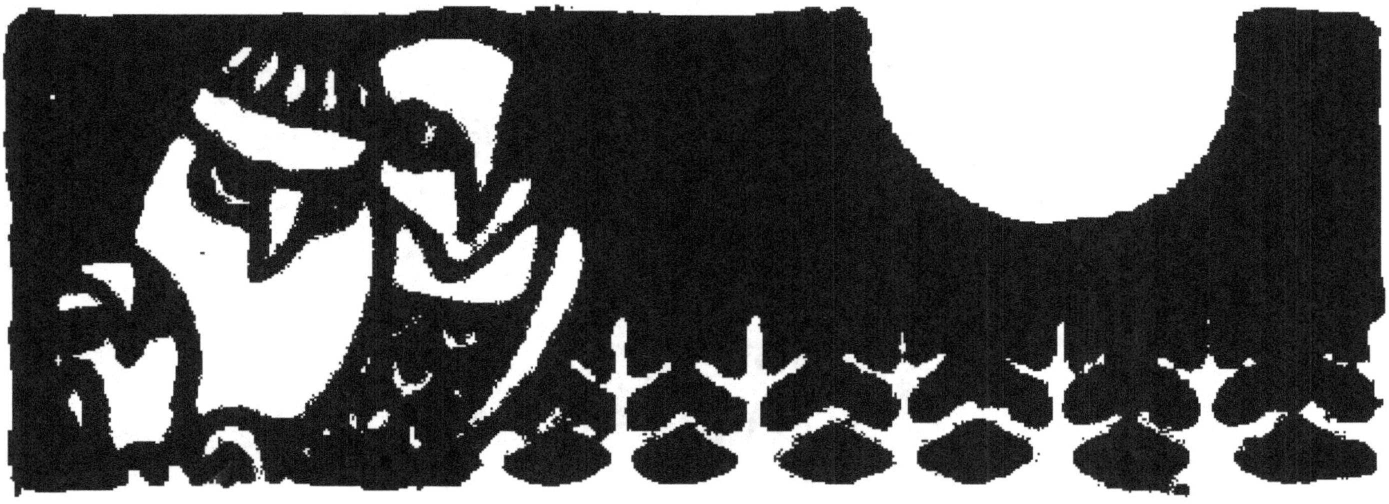

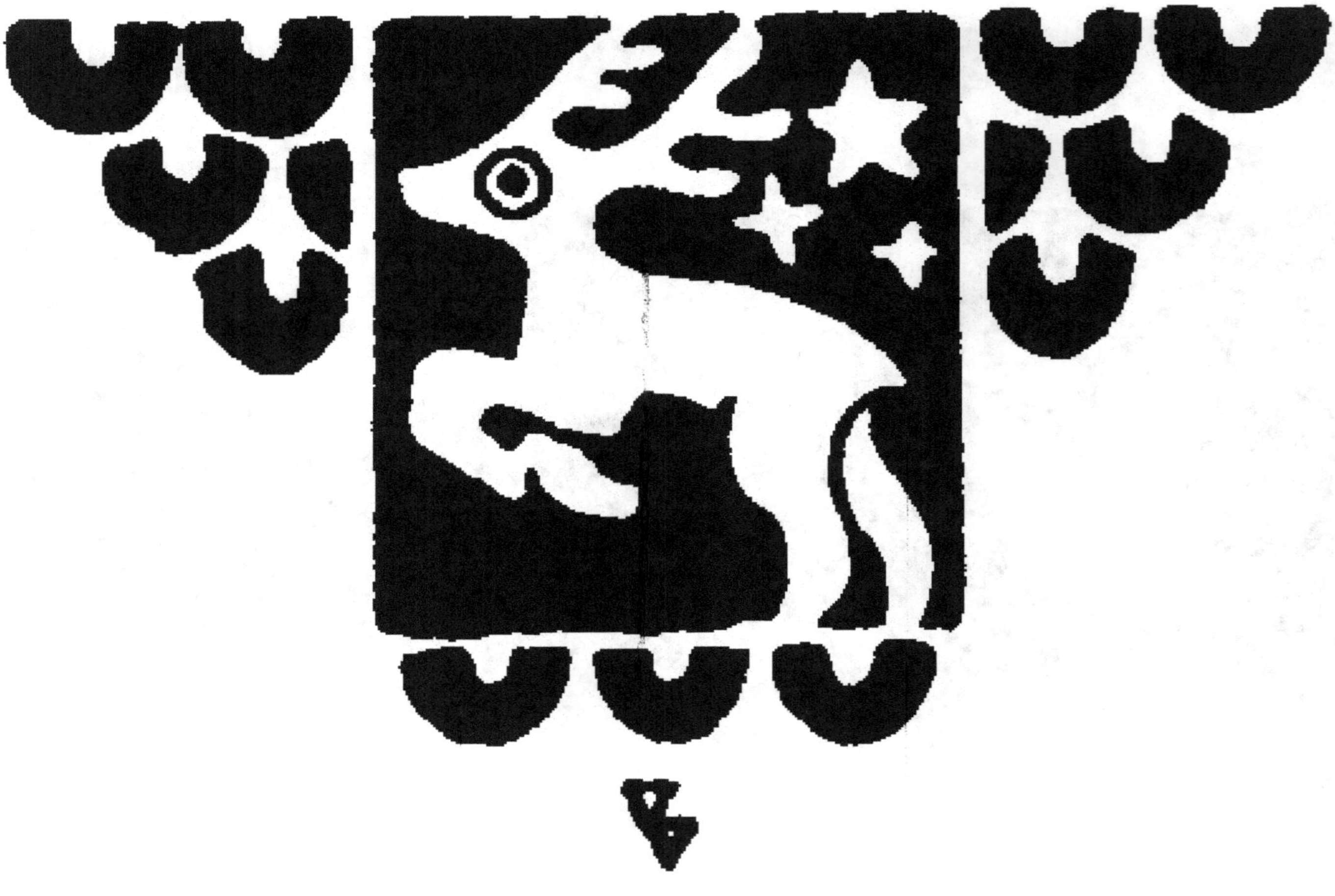

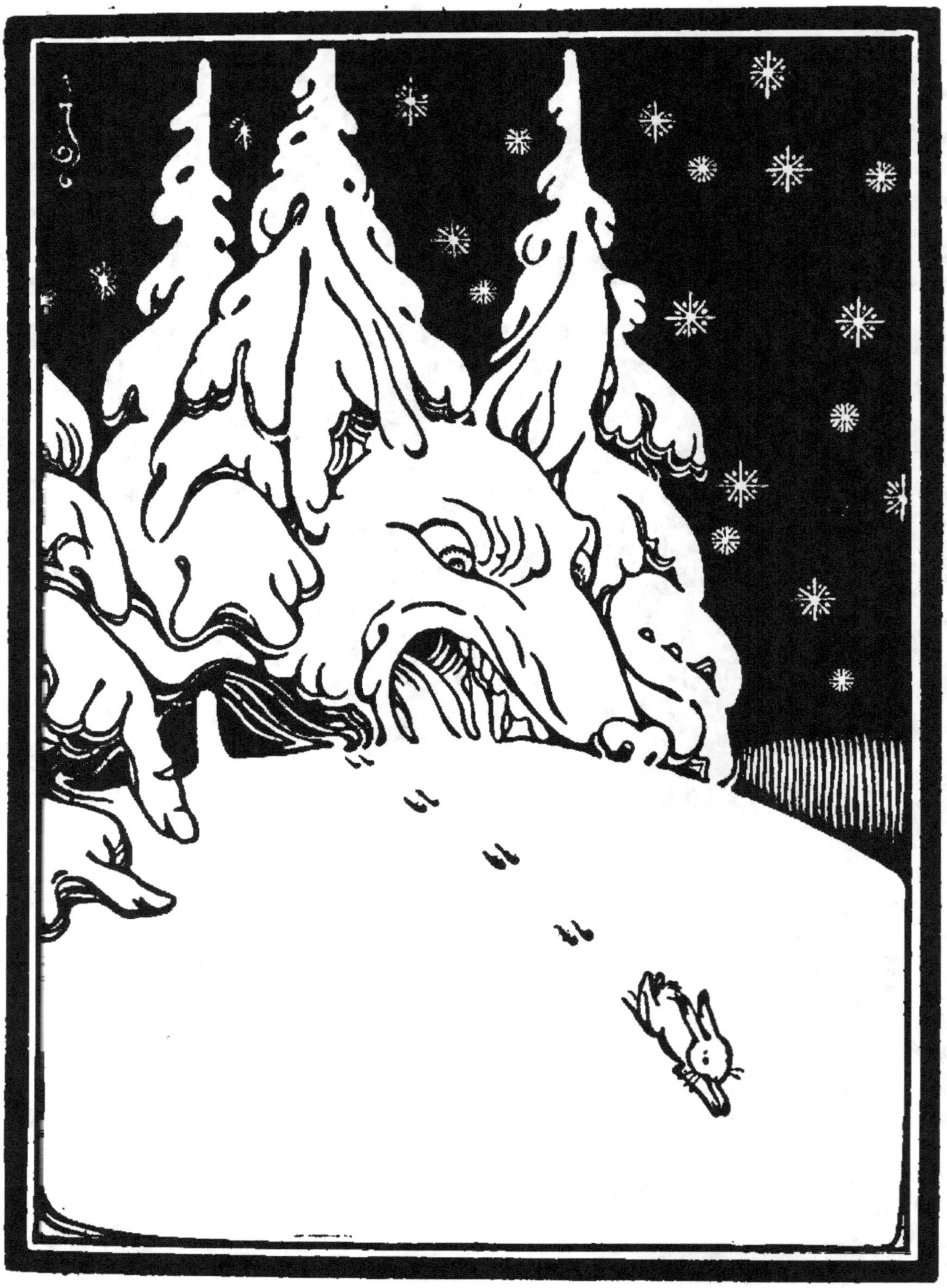

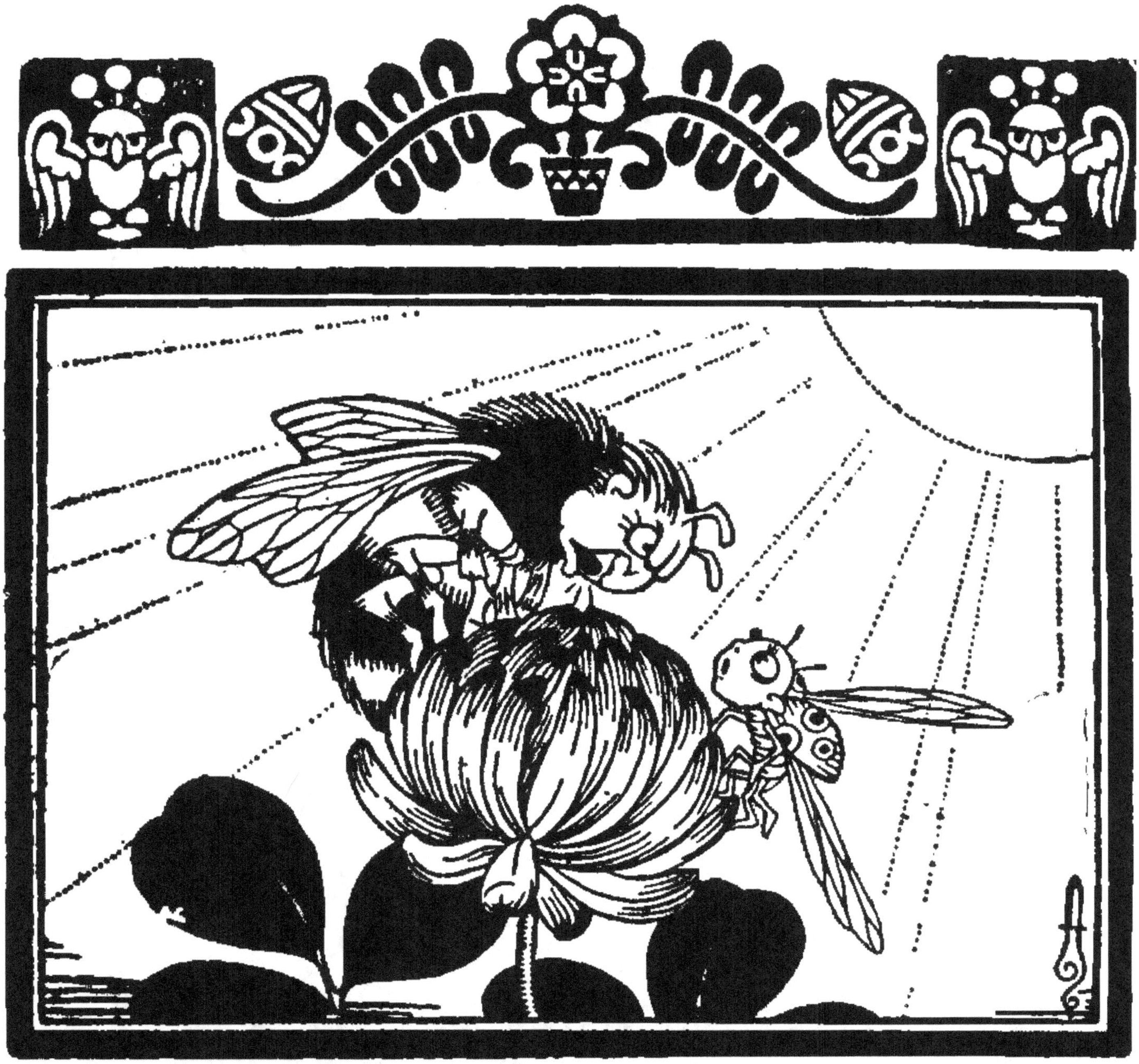

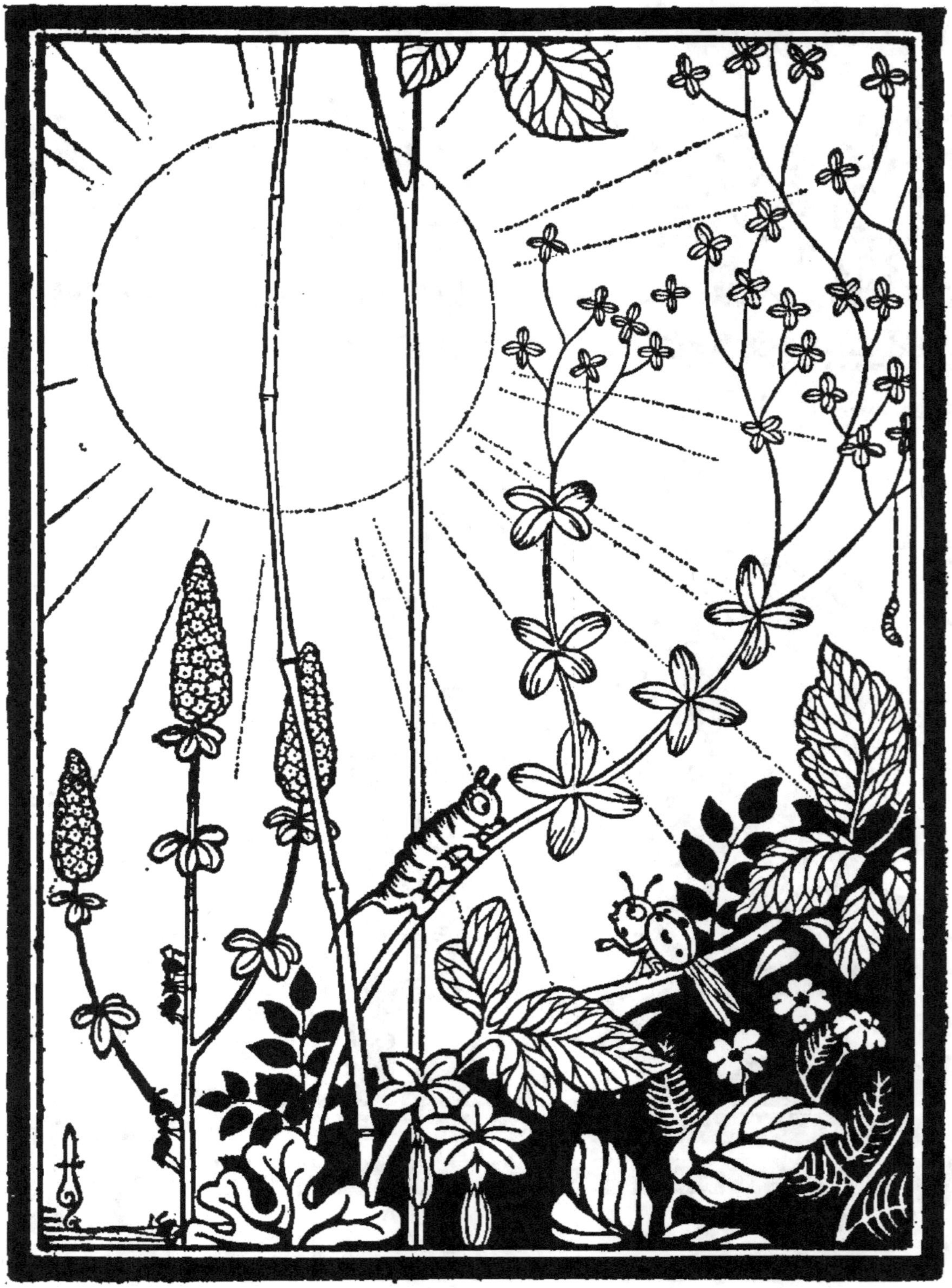

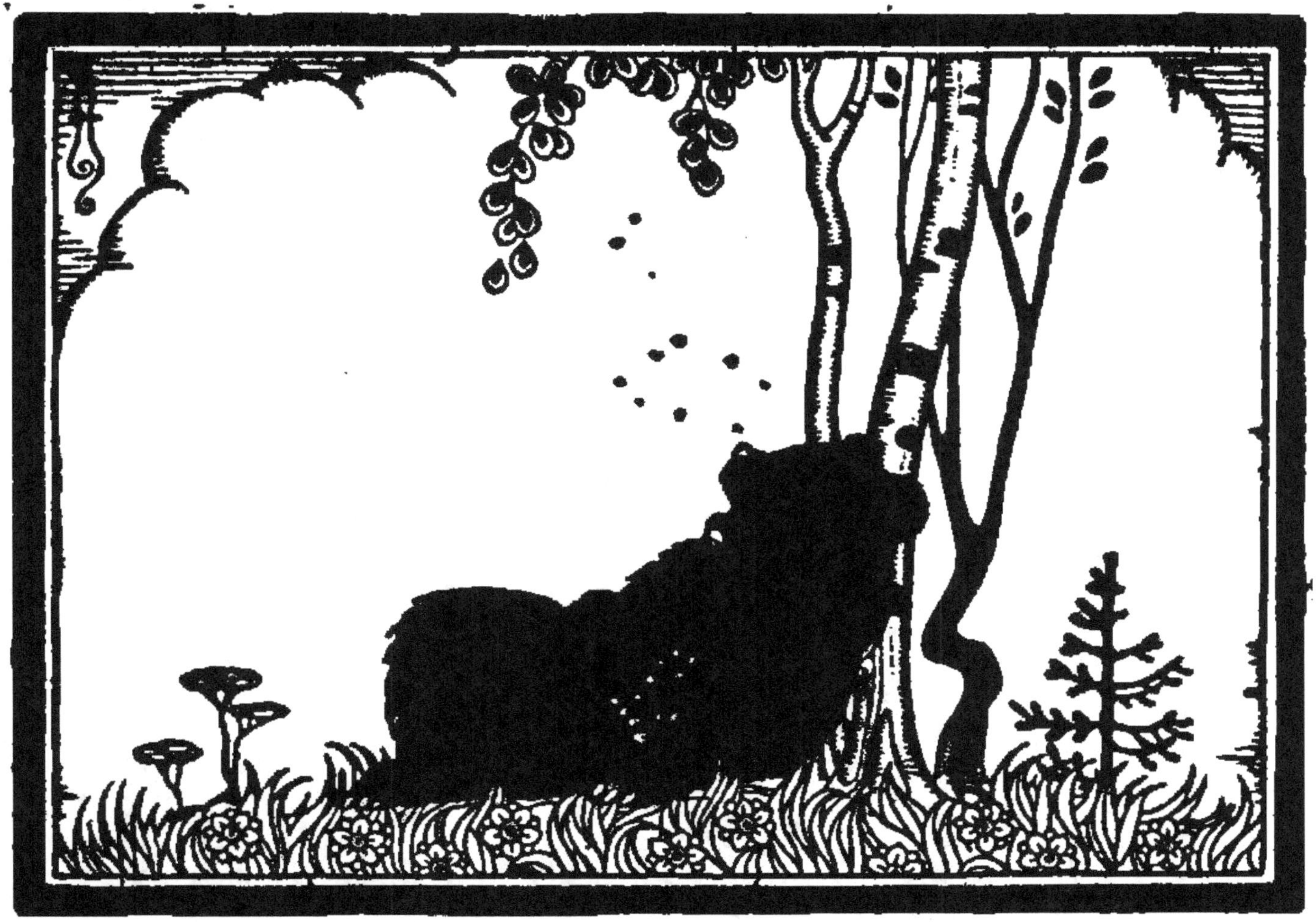

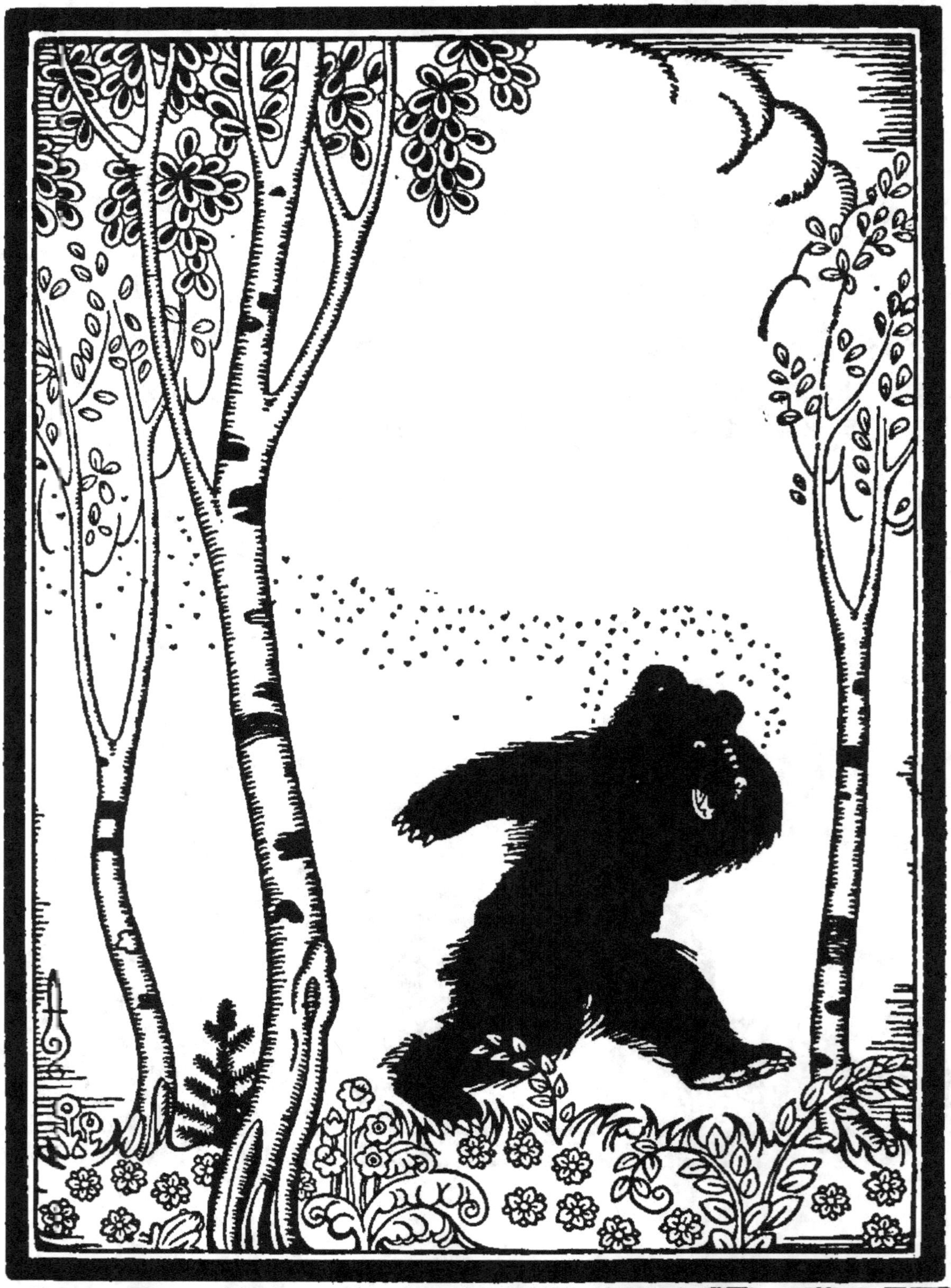

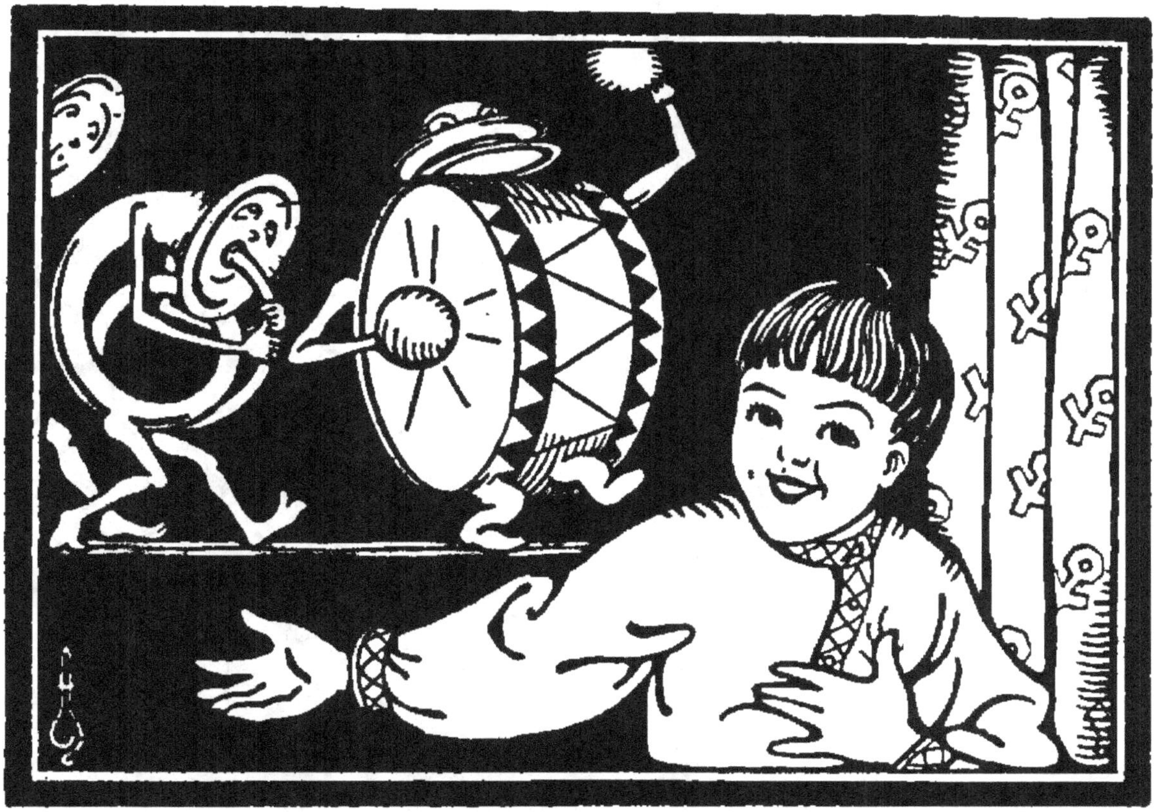

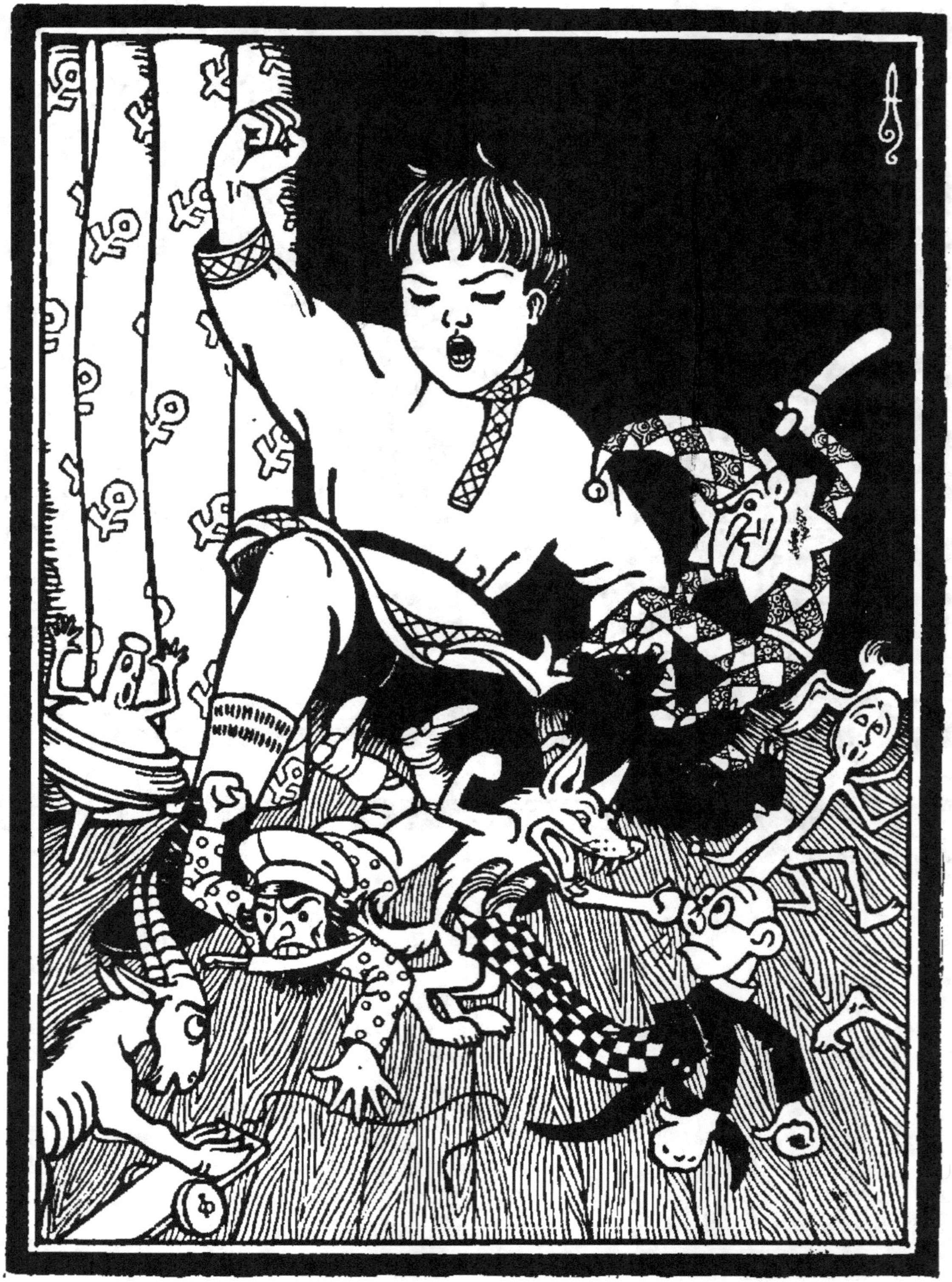

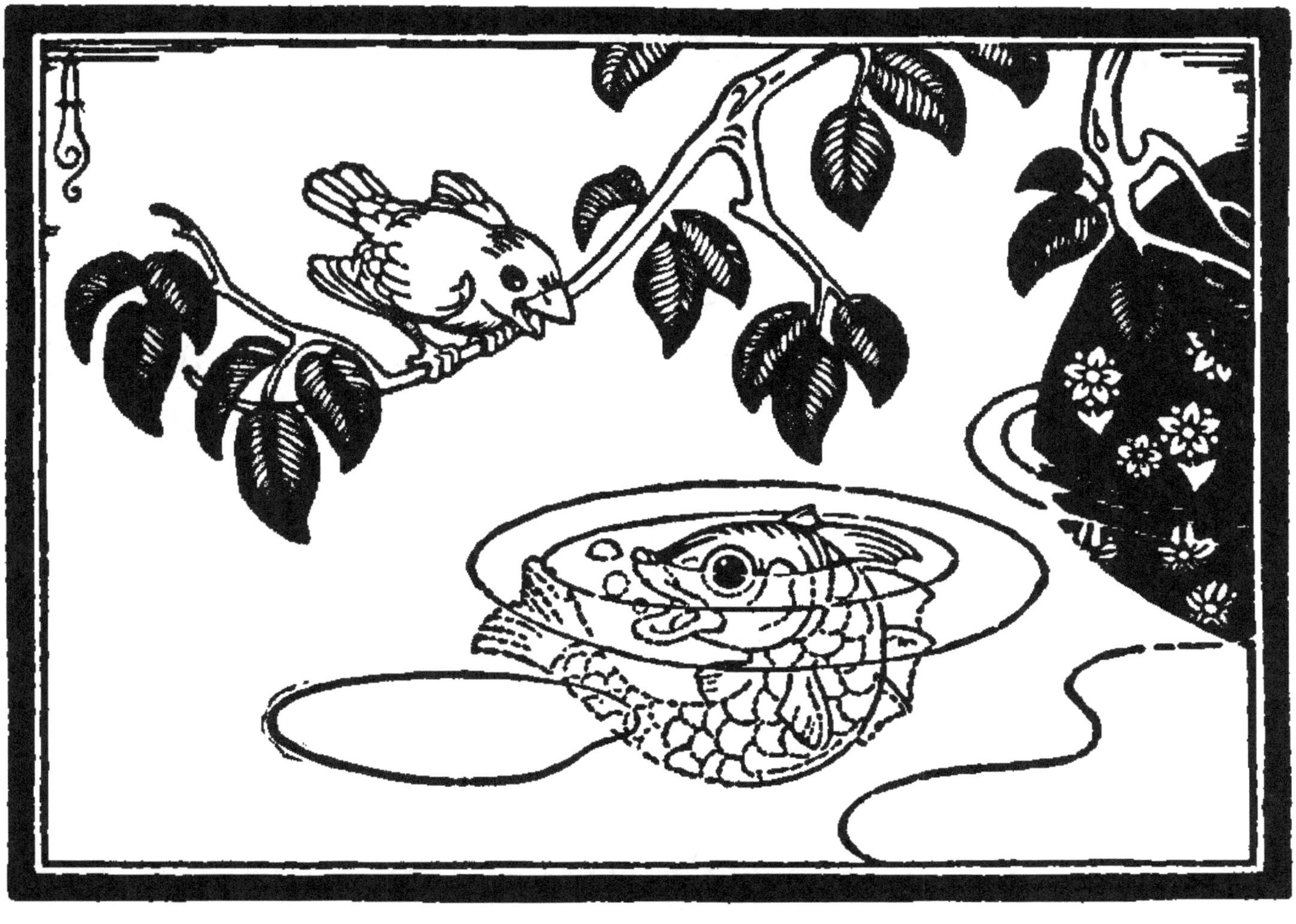

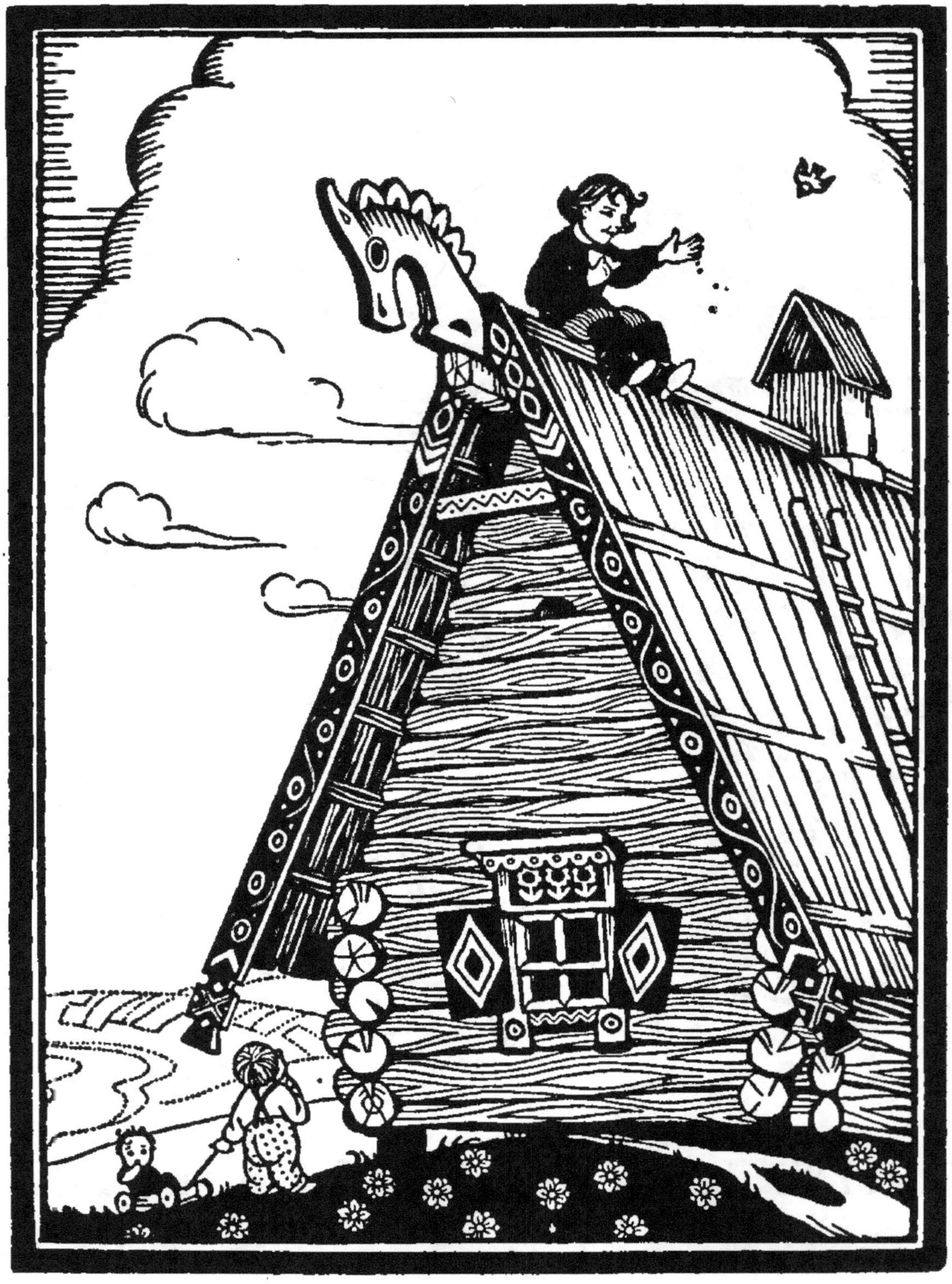

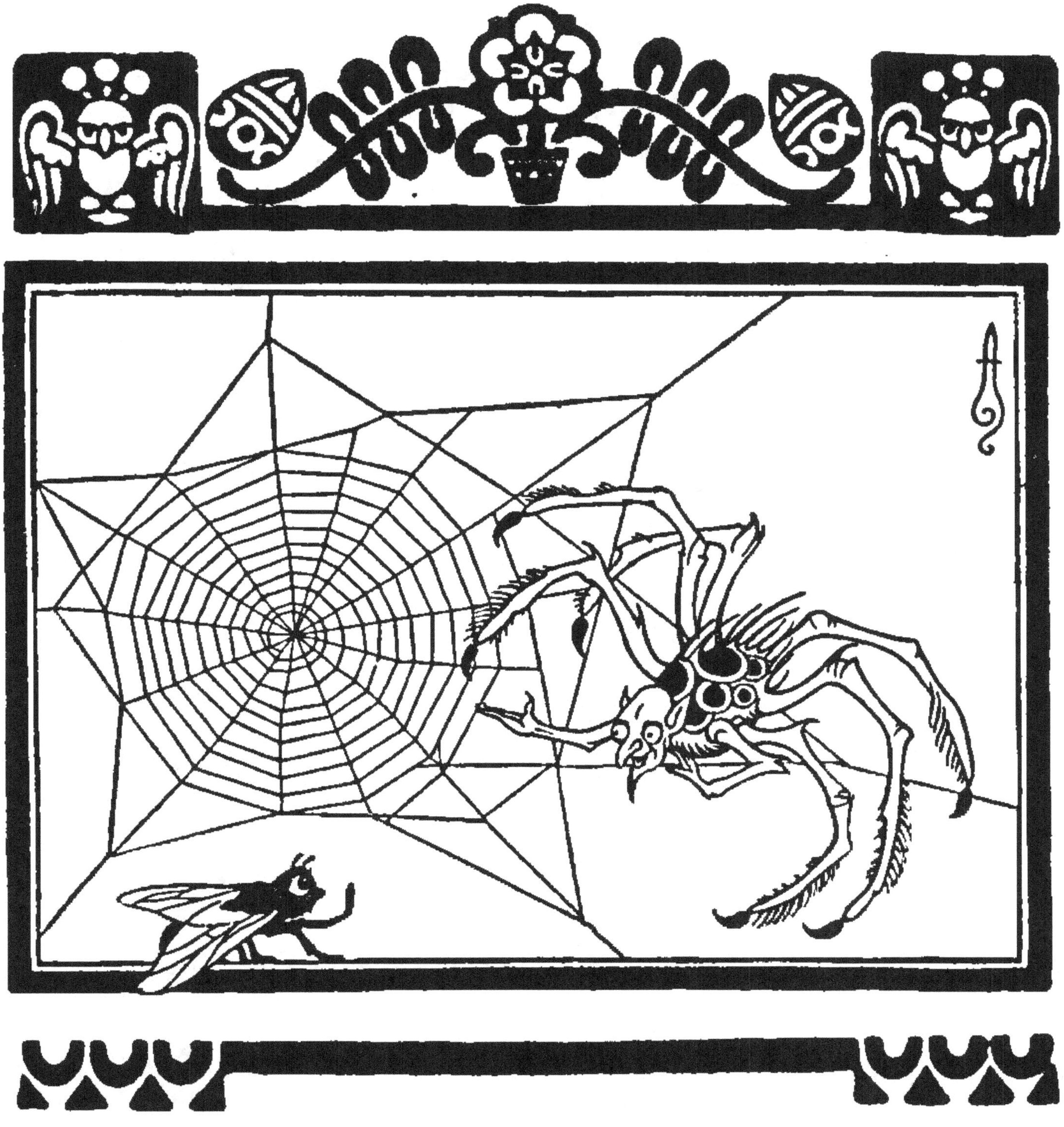

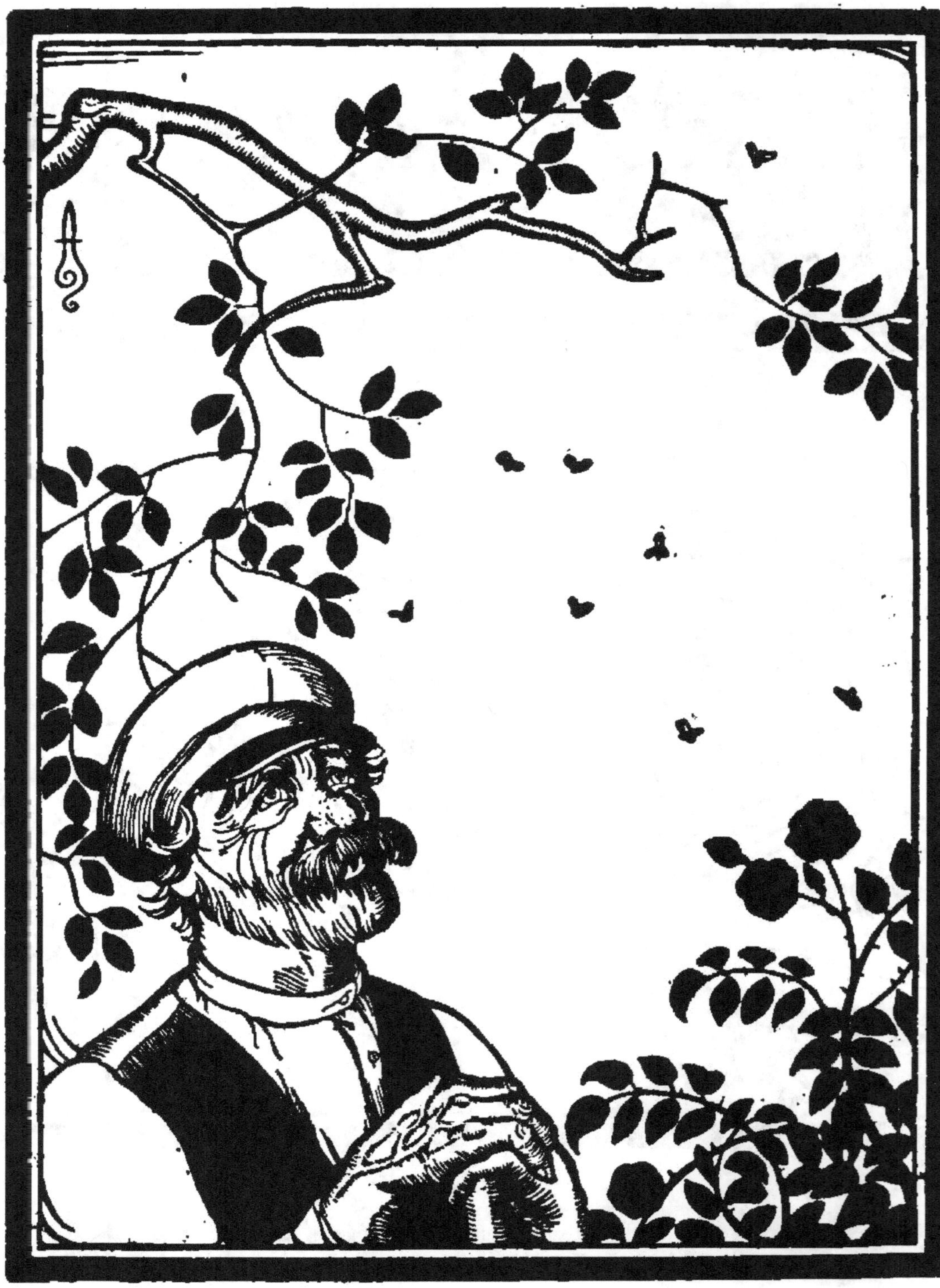

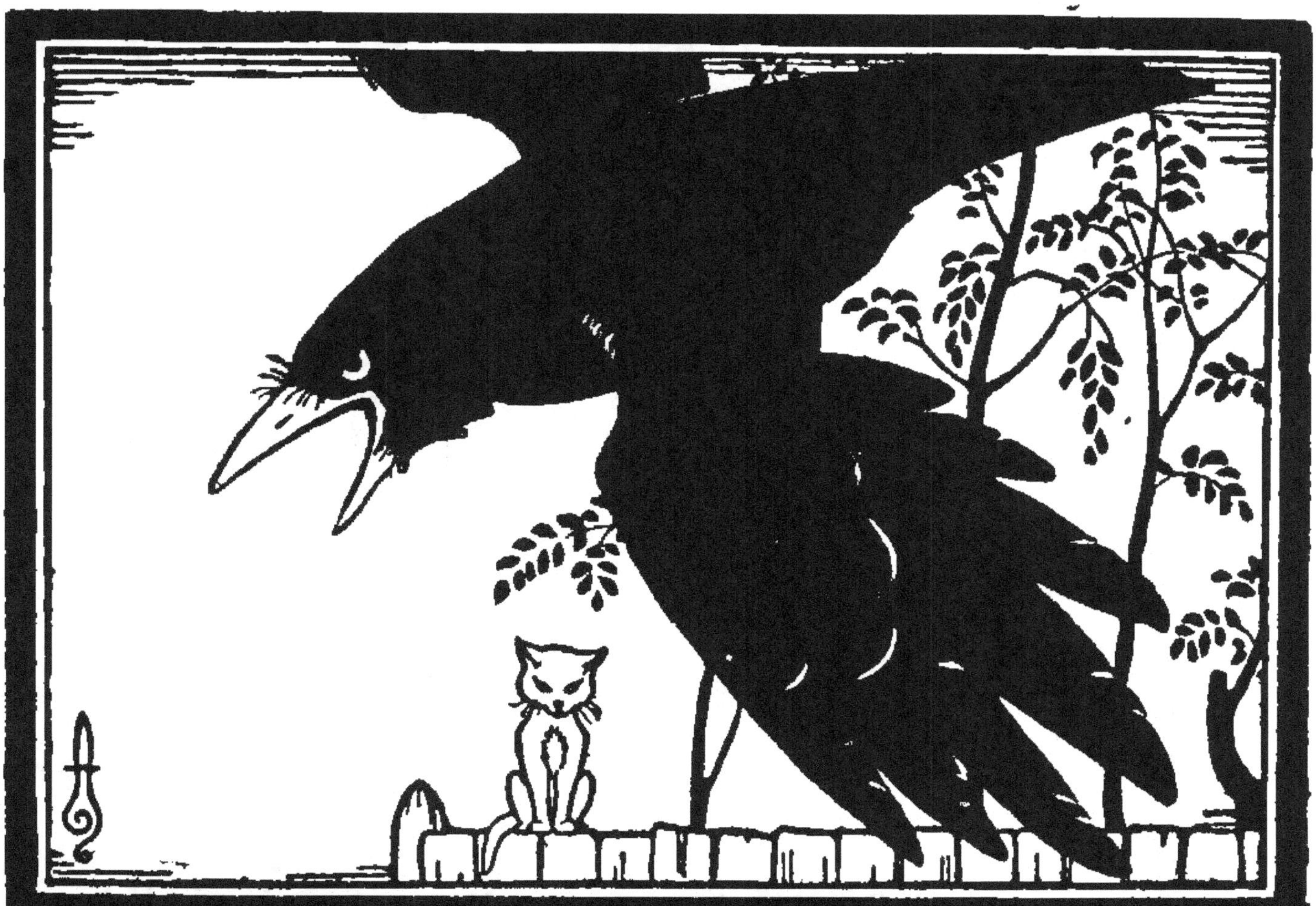

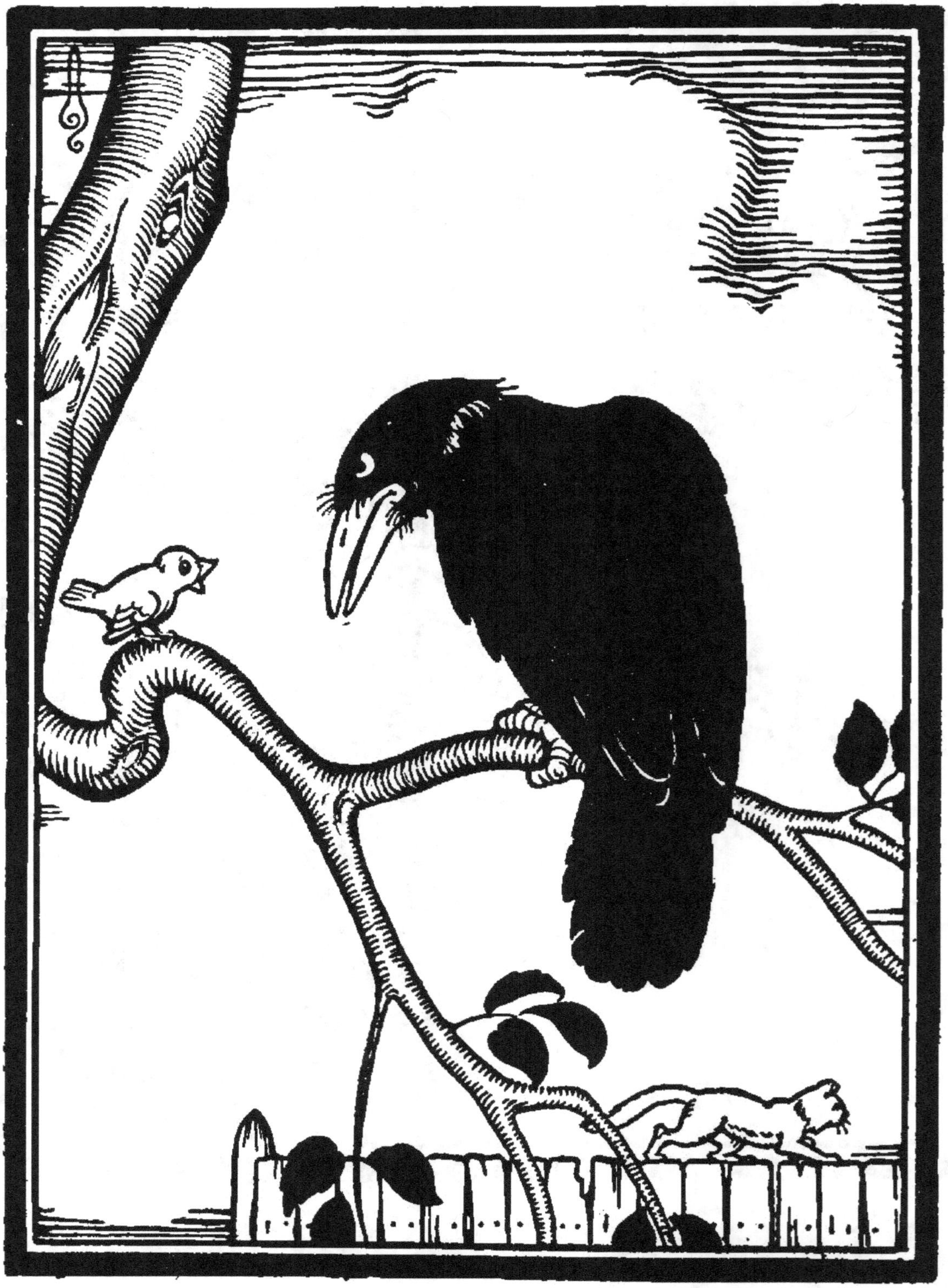

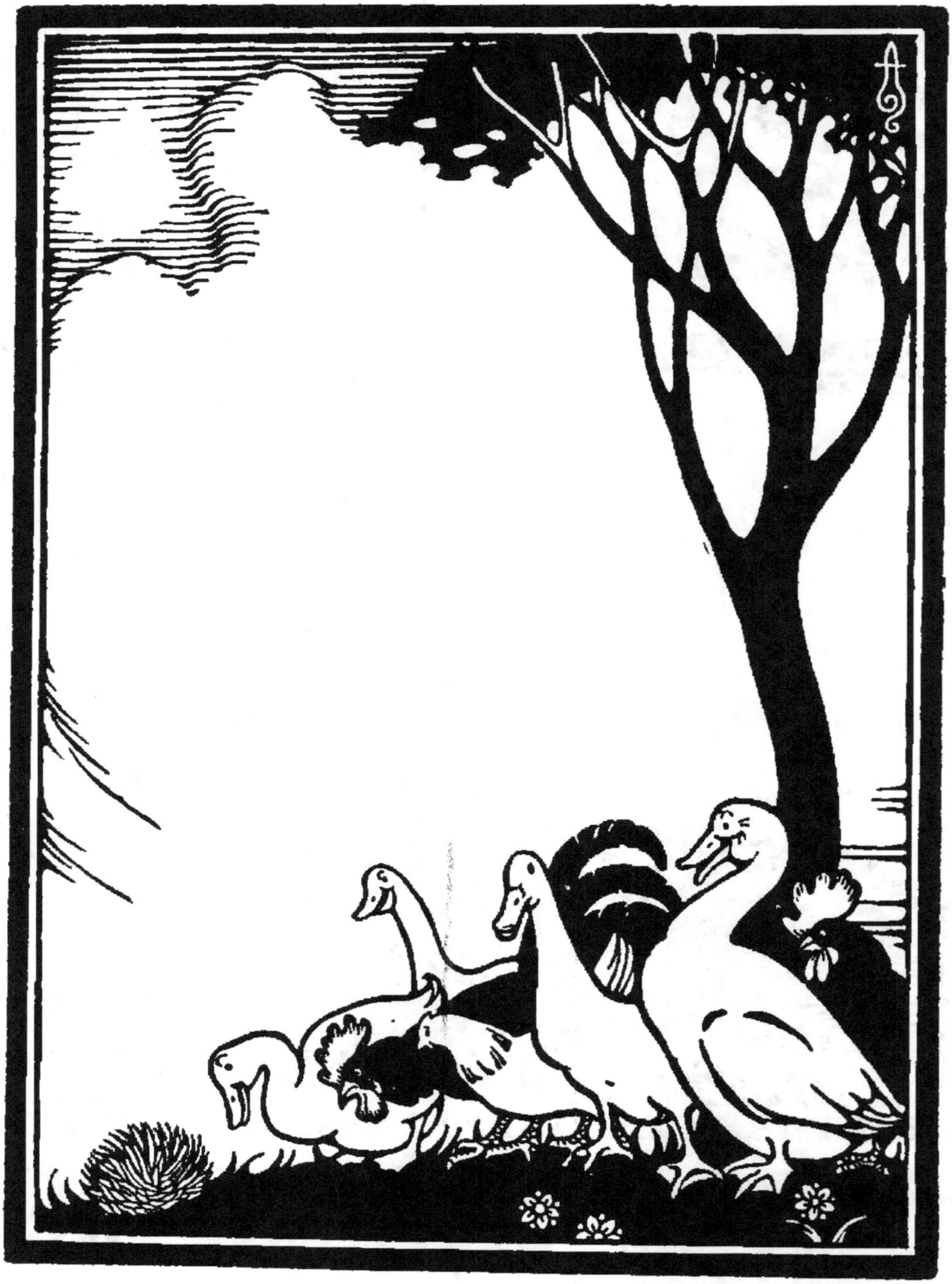

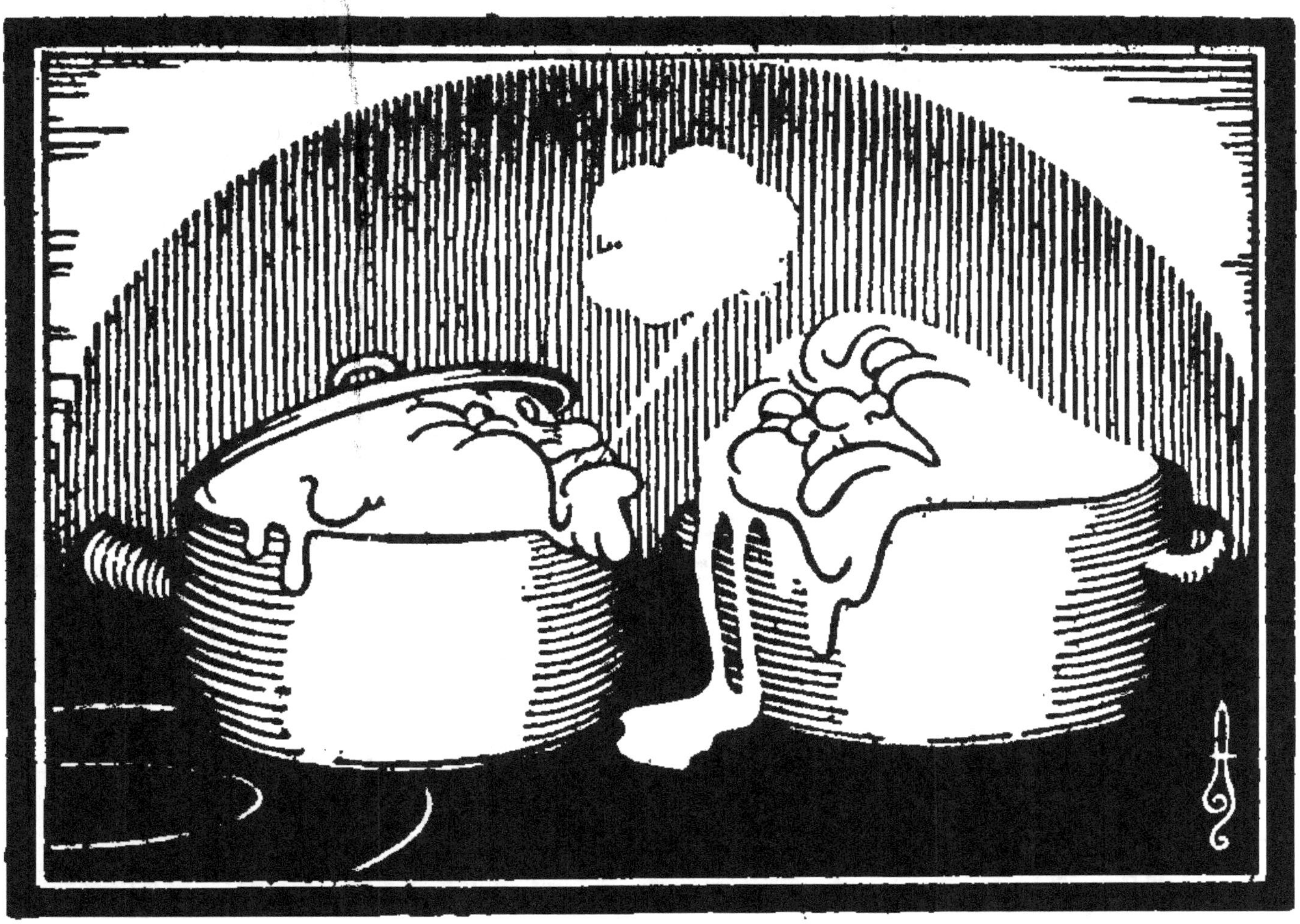

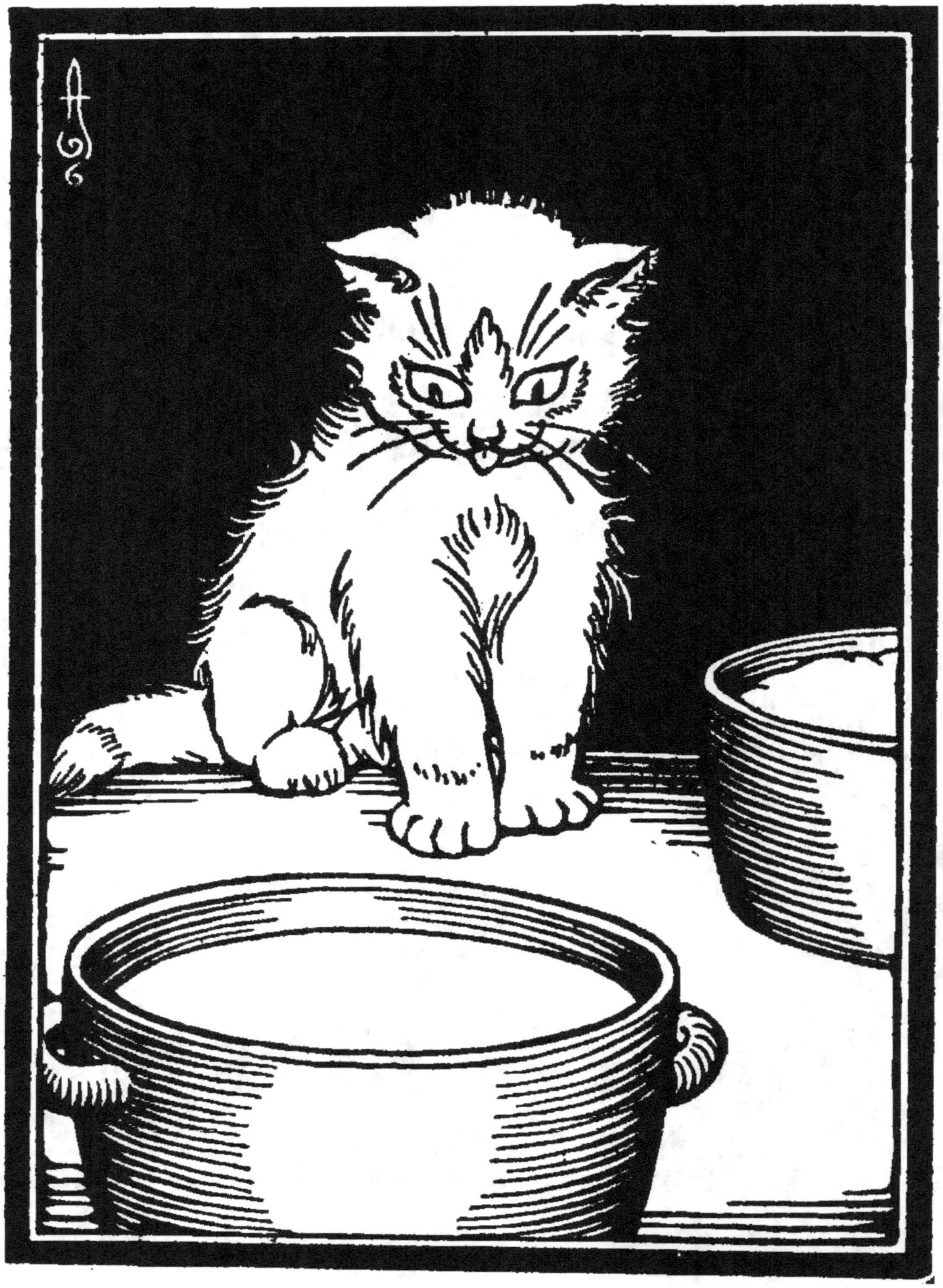

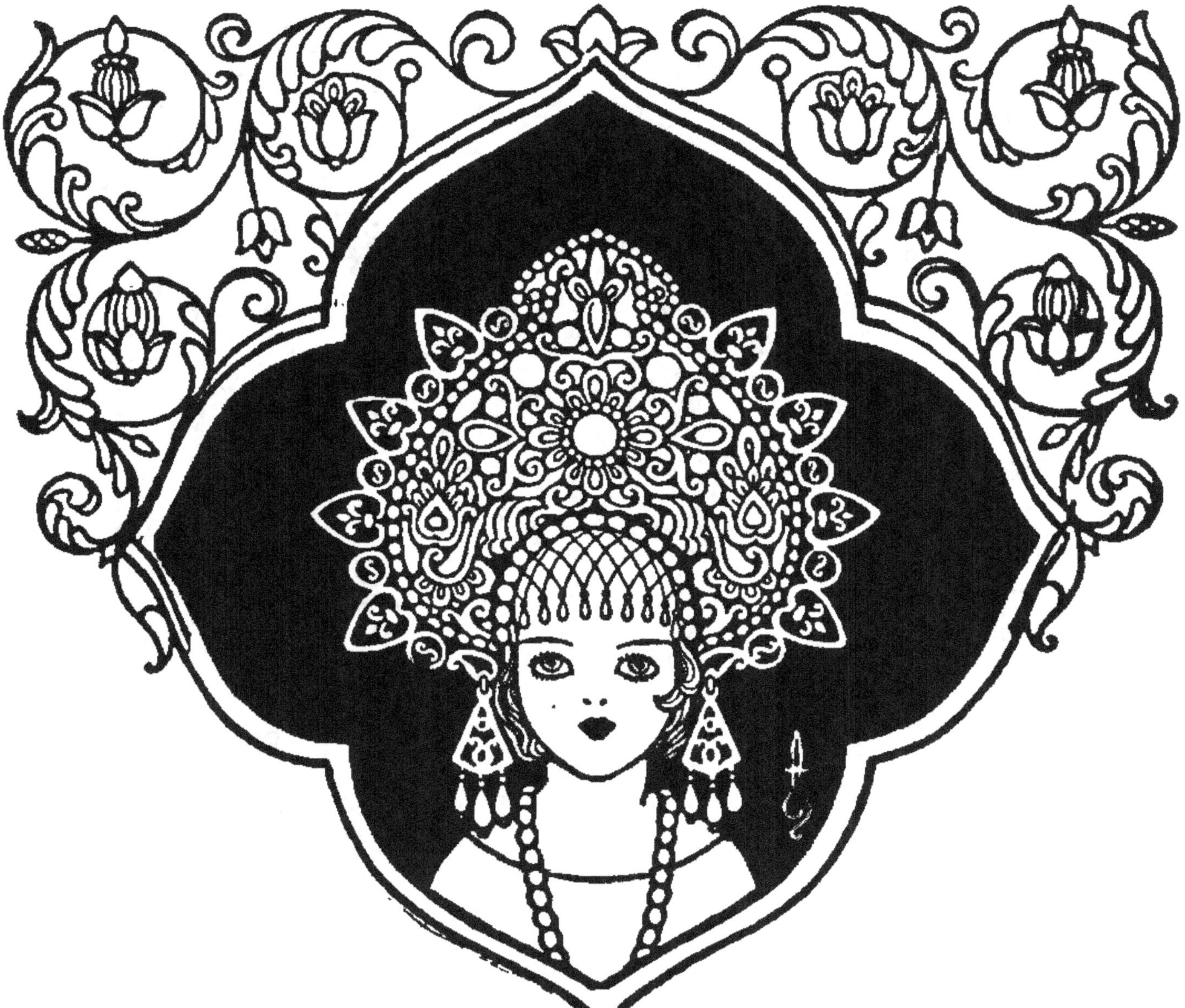

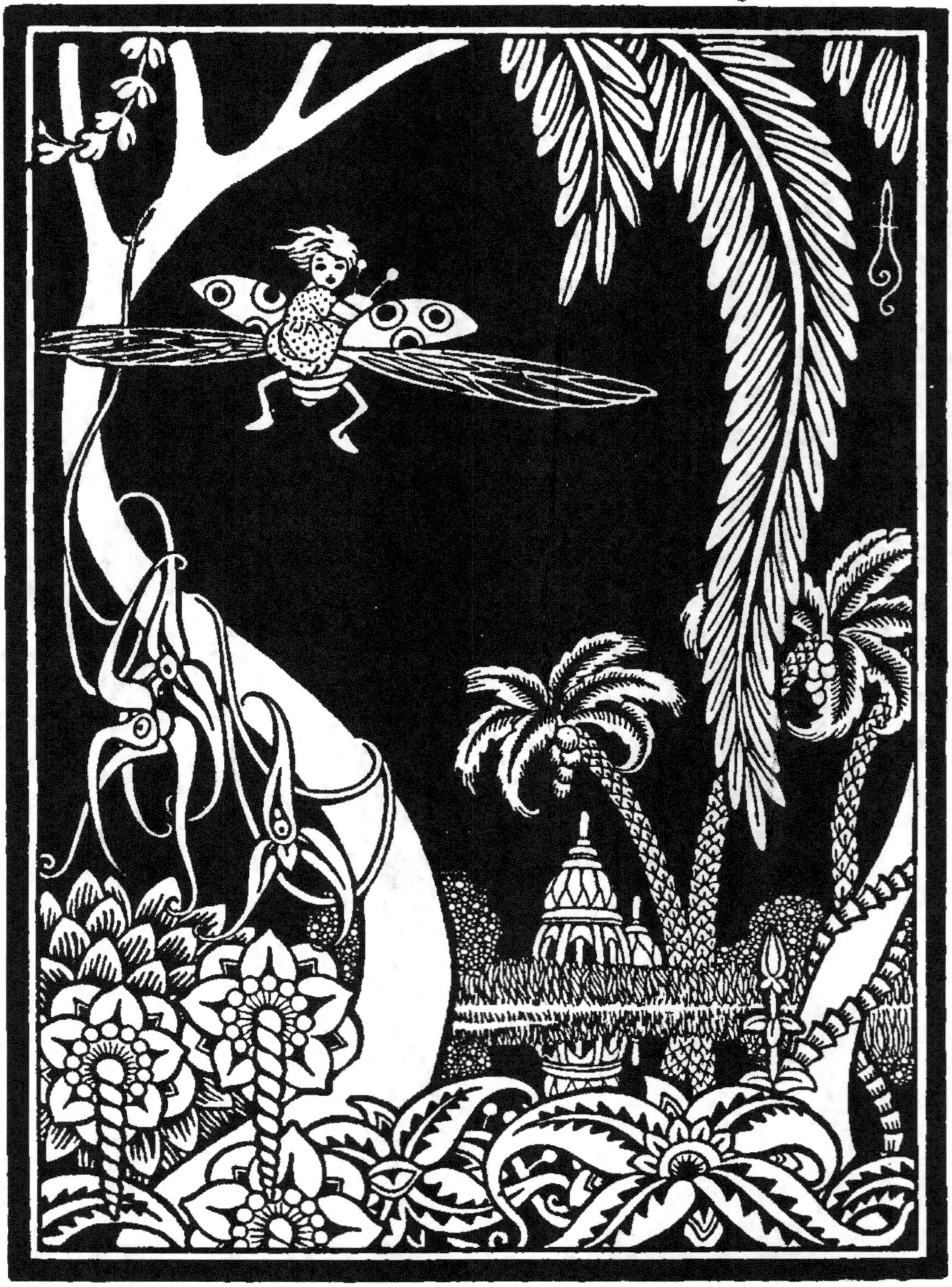

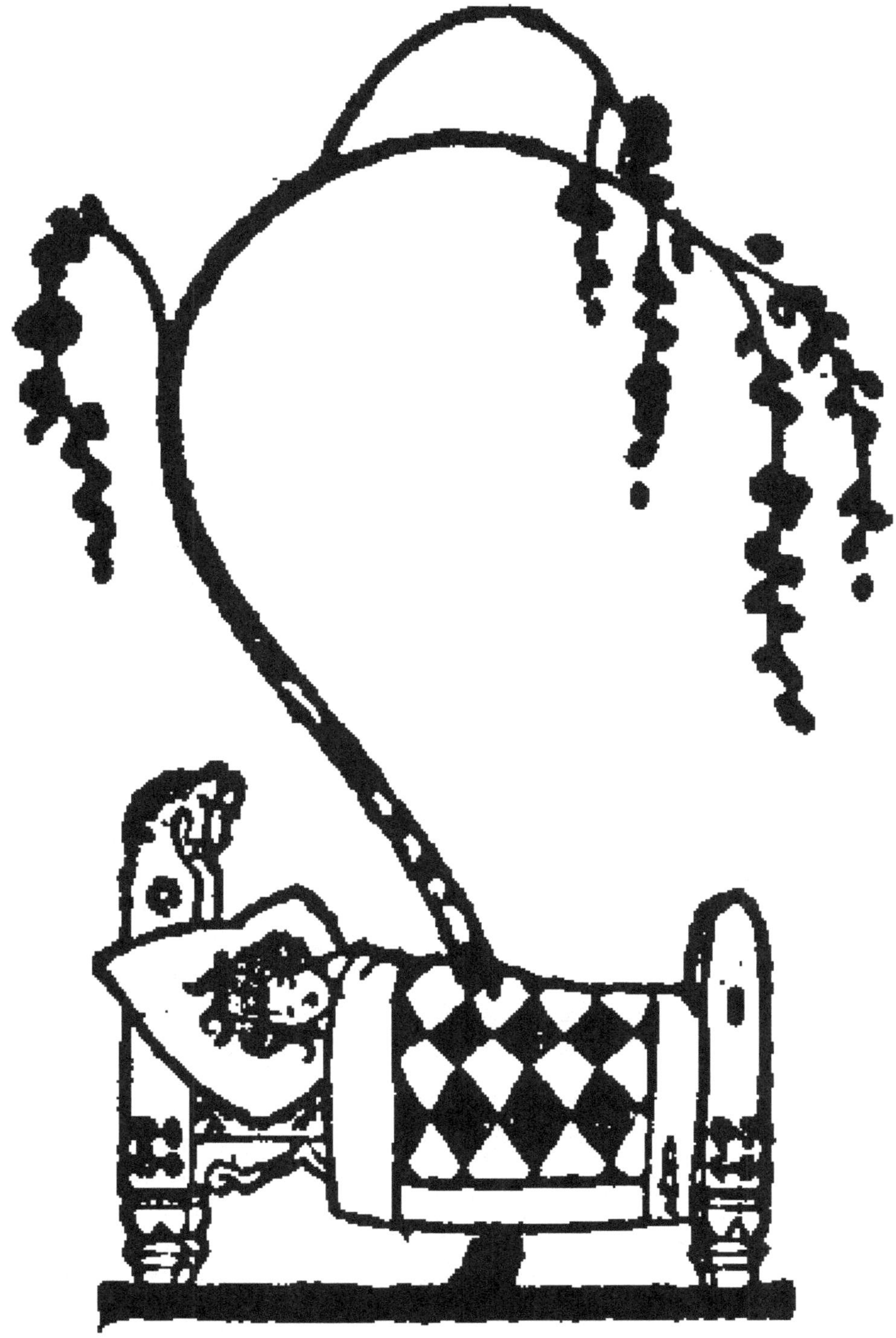

THE END

www.ingramcontent.com/pod-product-compliance
Lightning Source LLC
Chambersburg PA
CBHW082009230526
45468CB00023B/3031
*9781723080555*